SELF-ESTEEM
Workbook for Kids

SELF-ESTEEM
WORKBOOK for KIDS

40 Fun Activities to Feel Great about Yourself

TAIRA BURNS, LPC-MHSP

ILLUSTRATIONS BY CLAUDIO CERR

callisto
publishing
an imprint of Sourcebooks

Published by Callisto Publishing LLC C/O Sourcebooks LLC
P.O. Box 4410, Naperville, Illinois 60567-4410
(630) 961-3900
callistopublishing.com

This product conforms to all applicable CPSC and CPSIA standards.

Source of Production: 1010 Printing Asia Limited, Kwun Tong, Hong Kong, China
Date of Production: March 2024
Run Number: 5037705

Printed and bound in China.
OGP 10 9 8 7 6 5 4 3 2 1

CONTENTS

· ·

A LETTER TO
KIDS

Welcome!

Have you ever felt sad, angry, or low and just wanted to feel better? Maybe there are times when you don't feel so good about yourself or your abilities. This is called *unhealthy self-esteem*. It is something that everyone has experienced at some point in their life. When you have healthy self-esteem, you feel strong, confident, or brave. But when you experience unhealthy self-esteem, it can make life really hard. You might feel scared, sad, or alone. You can even experience healthy and unhealthy self-esteem at the same time!

As a professional counselor, I once worked with a kid who was new in town. They were so excited to make new friends and join a new cheerleading team. They had always felt like they had healthy self-esteem their whole life. When it came time for tryouts, though, they felt nervous and scared. They ended up not doing as well as they thought they would. If you have ever experienced unhealthy self-esteem, there are many things you can do to help feel better.

This book was created with you in mind. You will find 40 activities and exercises to help you build confidence and learn how to speak up for yourself. Each chapter of the book has different skills, tools, and activities to help boost your self-esteem. Start at the beginning and get ready to discover just how great you are!

A LETTER TO GROWN-UPS

. . . .

Welcome, parents and guardians!

This is a workbook designed for kids ages six to nine to help them get to know themselves, develop a positive self-image, boost self-esteem, and become more assertive in their everyday lives. Kids this age might experience different levels of stressors at school. These could be things like not feeling confident in math, or being called on in class and unsure of the answer. Kids this age also feel the pressure of fitting in with their peers and learning how to build friendships. In this book, you will find different activities that teach them how to identify their negative thoughts and change them to positive thoughts. Your child will learn to trust themselves more. They will also become more assertive when setting boundaries with things that might be impacting their self-esteem.

The activities, exercises, and practices are designed in a fun way to keep your child engaged while they learn. As your child works through the book, they will need your support. Part of building confidence and trusting yourself more is getting affirmations from those around you. This is where you come in. Support your child through each activity, and try to extend the lessons into everyday life. You may take a moment at the dinner table to practice deep breathing. Maybe you can practice gratitude together when you are shopping at the store. By finding these opportunities throughout the day, you are helping your child sustain the skills in real time.

Start at the beginning of the book, where your child will begin to learn more about self-esteem. Have fun as you help your child navigate the skills in the activities.

CHAPTER 1

Let's Talk about Self-Esteem

WHAT IS SELF-ESTEEM?

Imagine a kid who is really nervous about their upcoming math test. Just the thought of the test makes them feel like they have butterflies in their stomach. After they study and complete their flash cards, though, they start to feel more confident than ever. They go into their math test and ace it! They feel strong, smart, and proud of themselves. This is healthy self-esteem.

Self-esteem isn't anything you can touch or see. It is something that you feel inside your body. It's how much you value yourself as a person. Confidence and self-esteem go together like peanut butter and jelly. Confidence is a belief in your abilities—just like a kid truly believing they can ace their math test. Self-esteem is the feelings you have about yourself, like how this kid felt they were smart and strong.

There are two kinds of self-esteem. There is healthy self-esteem, which is when you feel good about yourself and respond to other people in positive ways. Then there is unhealthy self-esteem. If you are experiencing unhealthy self-esteem, you may feel scared, sad, or bad about yourself. Those negative feelings about your weaknesses turn into negative feelings about yourself. This may sometimes affect your life in not-so-great ways.

Check out the next exercise to find out more about healthy and unhealthy self-esteem.

SELF-ESTEEM CHECKLIST

What comes to mind when you think about healthy self-esteem? Look at the list of different thoughts. Underline the positive thoughts in green. Underline the negative thoughts in orange. If you have had any of these thoughts today, check the box.

☐ Why can't I be like them?

☐ I did my best.

☐ I am really good at this.

☐ I do not think I can do this.

☐ I am smart.

☐ They must think that I am not smart.

☐ I should never have worn this.

☐ I am proud of myself.

☐ It's probably my fault.

☐ I know what I am doing.

☐ I am the fastest runner.

☐ No one cares what I do.

How many thoughts were green?   - - - - - - - -

How many thoughts were orange?   - - - - - - -

How many boxes were checked?   - - - - - - -

If you checked more green than orange thoughts, you may be close to healthy self-esteem. If you checked more orange than green thoughts, you may be experiencing unhealthy self-esteem. Whatever you scored, keep reading through the book to build your self-esteem.

WHAT IS HEALTHY SELF-ESTEEM?

Having healthy self-esteem means that you feel good about yourself and your abilities. When you look in the mirror, you like what you see. Not only do you like what you see on the outside, but you also like what's on the inside. You like your thoughts, feelings, and choices. The beliefs you have about yourself are positive and uplifting. You might feel like you can achieve anything when you believe in yourself. A big part of healthy self-esteem is understanding who you are: your likes and dislikes, strengths and weaknesses, and talents.

Imagine that it's field day at school, and you are going to run a race. Instead of being scared or worried about what will happen, you believe you are going to do your best. You wake up that morning, put on your favorite shoes, and head out the door. When it comes time for the race, you give it your all—and you actually win first place! When you have healthy self-esteem, you have confidence in your abilities. This will sometimes affect the outcome, like how feeling good about yourself can help you win a race. In this next exercise, you are going to think about a time when you had healthy self-esteem.

REFLECTION

Kids with healthy self-esteem seem to enjoy life, make wise choices, and communicate well with others. Think about a time when you had healthy self-esteem. It could be a time you shared something with a friend on the playground. Maybe it was a time at home when you told a parent about your feelings. What were you doing? Who were you with? How did you feel? Write about it.

UNDERSTANDING UNHEALTHY SELF-ESTEEM

Imagine you are attending a new school. At your old school you had lots of friends and a great teacher. When you walk in the door of your new classroom, you feel uneasy. You think you won't make any friends. This is unhealthy self-esteem.

When you experience unhealthy self-esteem, you might have some unhelpful thoughts. These thoughts may come with big emotions. You might feel frustrated, scared, or even a little sad. You might want to scream, throw a toy, or hit someone you care about. When you have big emotions, you might have big reactions. Has this ever happened to you?

It is normal to have unhelpful thoughts and feelings. But when these not-so-good emotions stay around for too long, they will create unhealthy self-esteem. The next few exercises will help you learn about yourself so you can build healthy self-esteem.

ALL ABOUT ME

It's time to think about someone special: you! Finish each sentence by drawing a picture in the box.

1. **I feel happy when I...**

2.   **My friends would say I am the best at...**

continued »»

3. My family thinks that I am awesome because...

4. Something that I am proud of is...

BUBBLING UP

Knowing what you really think about yourself will help you understand your self-esteem. The way you think about yourself shows up in everyday life. Maybe you feel like you are not athletic. This might show up in gym class when you play games. Or maybe you feel like you are not smart enough. This might show up in other classes.

What do you think about yourself? What do you like about yourself? Look at the words in the bubbles. Circle the bubbles that best describe you.

Now count your bubbles. How many did you circle? _ _ _ _ _ _ _ _ _ _ _ _ _ _ _ _ _ _ _

If you counted seven or more bubbles, your self-esteem is healthy. If you counted fewer than seven bubbles, you may have unhealthy self-esteem. Think about this as you keep working through the book.

In the blank bubbles below, write words that describe how you would like to feel about yourself.

SELF-ESTEEM AND ME

Self-esteem can change your whole life. When you are experiencing unhealthy self-esteem, it doesn't just affect you. It affects all the people you interact with. What if you were invited to a party where you didn't know any other guests? If you are a person with unhealthy self-esteem, you might not feel good about yourself and might have unhelpful thoughts about meeting new people. When someone introduces themself, you might feel nervous and not respond. You may even just walk away. This behavior comes from unhealthy self-esteem. The way we act affects our relationships with people who care about us.

When you have unhealthy self-esteem, you may experience fear or anxiety. Anxiety can feel like butterflies in your stomach that won't stop fluttering around. Everyone experiences anxiety at times. It can be normal to feel anxiety before meeting a new friend or getting a new teacher at school. But unhealthy self-esteem can cause anxiety, too. So far, you have been getting to know yourself a little better. This is one of the first steps to boosting your self-esteem. In the next few exercises, you are going to learn to love yourself by exploring your strengths and weaknesses.

WHAT I LIKE ABOUT ME

When you think about yourself, you might think about how you look on the outside. Maybe you like your hair or your eye color. But your beauty is more than just your appearance. Look inside yourself to notice your personality and how you treat others. Think about what special talents you have. What have you have achieved in school or outside of school? If you were to ask your friends to describe you, what would they say? Name five things that you like about yourself. Include qualities on the outside and, most important, the inside.

1. ---

2. ---

3. ---

4. ---

5. ---

I'M AMAZING!

You are an amazing person inside and out. Fill in the blanks to complete each sentence about how great you are.

1. **I am amazing because** _____

   _____

2. **My friends think I am amazing because** _____

   _____

3. **I like who I am because** _____

   _____

4. **I am really good at** _____

   _____

5. My greatest talent is _

    _

6. I feel happiest when _

    _

7. Somewhere I feel happy is _

    _

8. Someone who makes me feel happy is _

    _

MY SAFE PLACE

When you are overwhelmed with big feelings, do you ever want to escape? If you could escape, where would you go? It's probably a place that makes you feel happy and safe. You might feel safest in your bedroom. Or maybe you feel calmest when you are on the beach near the ocean. What about the mountains, where you can feel the cold air on your face? Think about your safe space. Now draw a picture of it.

5, 4, 3, 2, 1

Picture yourself in the safe place from the previous exercise. Now close your eyes and imagine that you are physically there. What can you see, hear, smell, taste, or touch? Read the prompts and write about what you feel.

Name five things you can see.

1. _____

2. _____

3. _____

4. _____

5. _____

continued »»

Name four things you can touch.

1. ---

2. ---

3. ---

4. ---

Name three things you can hear.

1. ---

2. ---

3. ---

Name two things you can smell.

1. ---

2. ---

Name one thing you can taste.

1. ---

CHAPTER 2

All about Me

KNOWING MYSELF

There are billions of people in the world, and each person is different. There are some things that people have in common, and there are some things that are specific only to you. The combination of these things is what makes you unique. Be proud of who you are! There might be times when you don't feel so good about yourself, and you may not even like yourself. These times can be hard. Getting to know yourself is the first step toward liking who you are and building your self-esteem.

What are you good at? You are probably good at many things. These are your strengths. You could be really good at dancing, basketball, science, or anything! It's also important to learn about the things you are not so good at. You could call these your weaknesses. You may not be good at everything you have tried, and that's okay. Everyone has strengths and weaknesses. That's what makes each person unique.

GETTING TO KNOW MYSELF

Fill in the blanks to complete each statement. This will help you explore more about yourself.

My favorite color is _____

I have this many pets: _____

My favorite food is _____

I want to be _____ when I grow up.

I am really good at _____

My favorite thing about myself is _____

_____

MY TALENTS

Everyone has certain talents where they really shine. Some kids are good at softball, tennis, or soccer. Other kids might be good at singing, dancing, or acting. You could also be good at painting, video games, or solving puzzles. When you focus on your talents, it makes you feel good about yourself. When you feel good about yourself, it will boost your self-esteem.

The cool thing about talent is that it can grow and change over time. As you grow, your strengths and weaknesses might shift. You might enjoy singing right now, but as you get older your talent in dancing might grow stronger. Explore your special talents in this next exercise to continue building your self-esteem.

TALENT SHOW

You have so many talents and skills that you haven't discovered yet. These hidden gems are just waiting to be uncovered. You might already know the things you are good at. There may also be things that you are interested in trying someday. Write out all the things you love to do already or would be interested in trying.

Now draw a picture of yourself trying one of these new activities or talents below.

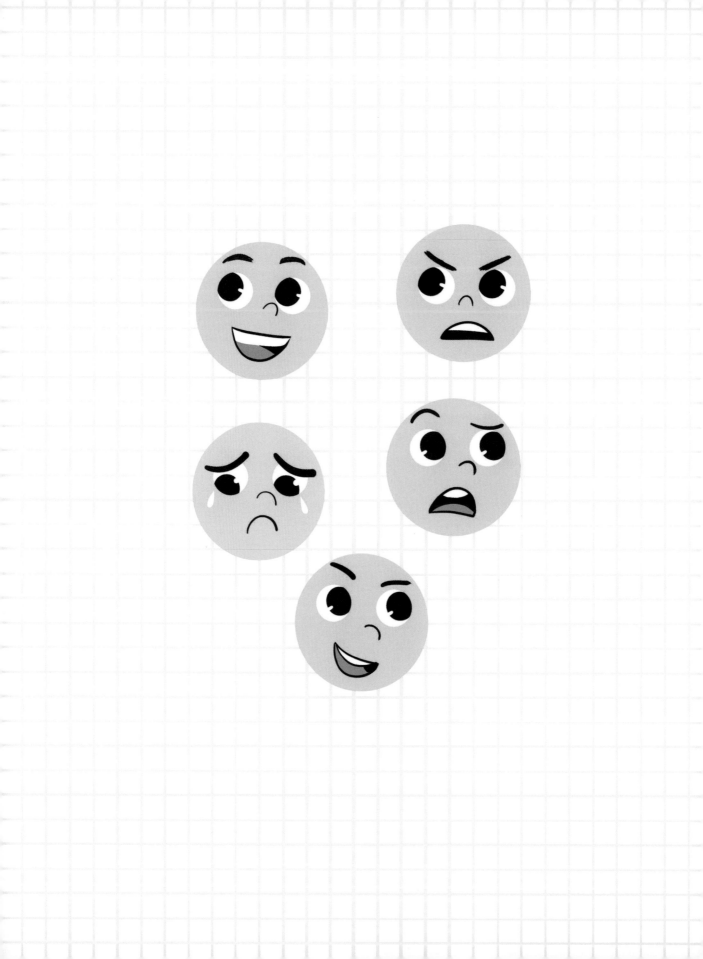

MY FEELINGS

Everyone has lots of different feelings. There are feelings that feel good, like happiness, pride, excitement, and joy. Then there are feelings that feel not so good, like sadness, anger, or fear. When you have not-so-good feelings too often, it may create unhealthy self-esteem.

How would you feel if a younger sibling broke your favorite toy or lost your favorite stuffed animal? You might feel sad, frustrated, or even angry. When things like this happen, try to take a moment and count to 10. You are taking a break before you react. Taking this time to pause sends a message to your not-so-good feelings. You could also try singing or listening to your favorite song. Music can be a way to take a break and do something that makes you happy. When you pause to do something that you enjoy, it lets your not-so-good feelings know that you are not ready to react. Check out these activities to learn more strategies that help with the not-so-good feelings.

WHAT IS AROUND YOU?

When you experience not-so-good feelings, taking a pause can sometimes help. Look around when you pause. Notice all the things that are happening. Are you in your home? You may hear a bird outside your window. You may hear music from the next room. You may smell delicious food cooking. Once you notice what is taking place around you, you'll start to focus your attention on those things. This can help you focus on the good things happening around you. By pausing and looking at your surroundings, you are helping your not-so-good feelings turn into good feelings.

Taking a moment to look around you is an important strategy to have in your self-esteem tool kit. Try it now! Write the first letter of your name in the box below and decorate it.

Now look around you. Write down everything you see that starts with the first letter of your name.

BUBBLE BREATHING

Here's something to try when you feel not so good. Imagine that you are blowing a bubble. Take a deep breath in. As you slowly breathe out, watch the bubble carry your not-so-good feelings away. When you breathe deeply and imagine your troubles floating away, it can help you feel calm, relaxed, and even happy. Now draw a picture of you blowing your worry bubble away in the box below.

MY TRIGGERS

Triggers are thoughts, words, or actions that cause not-so-good feelings. Everyone can have triggers, and they may be different for each person. Say that you sit in the same spot in class every day. Then one day, a classmate takes your spot and laughs at you. You might feel upset or angry. The trigger here is the classmate taking your spot and then laughing. A trigger is something that causes you to feel an emotion. Once you know what your triggers are, it can help you cope with the not-so-good feelings that follow them.

A *comfort zone* is where you feel safe and at ease. A lot of people like to stay in their comfort zone, because it helps them avoid their triggers. Think about the classmate stealing your spot in class. If you were to stay in your comfort zone, you might avoid asking them to move or avoid telling a teacher. You might just find a new place to sit. As you learn a little more about your triggers, you'll also learn about your comfort zone. For example, hunger can be a trigger. Every time you are hungry, you might begin to feel angry or frustrated. Since you know this is a trigger for you, you can ask an adult for a snack to avoid feeling angry or frustrated. Taking action and doing something when you know you are triggered can help you manage those not-so-good feelings.

WHAT PUSHES YOUR BUTTONS?

Experiencing a trigger is also known as having your buttons pushed. You can be triggered or have your buttons pushed at any time. You may or may not know when it's going to happen. Look at the list of common buttons that get pushed. When something pushes your buttons or triggers you, you might have a big emotion like anger, sadness, frustration, or fear. This will sometimes cause you to yell, scream, cry, or even throw an object. Circle the things that really push your buttons. Feel free to add any triggers that are not on the list by writing them on the blank lines provided.

BEING TOLD ON

BEING IGNORED

LOUD NOISES

LOSING A GAME

AN ACCIDENT HAPPENING

BEING LEFT OUT

BAD NEWS

CHEATING

WAITING AWHILE

BEING HUNGRY

BEING TOUCHED

UNFAIR TREATMENT

TESTS OR GRADES

BEING LATE

BEING TIRED

BEING TOLD WHAT TO DO

NOT UNDERSTANDING WHAT TO DO

THINGS NOT GOING AS PLANNED

BEING BULLIED

WHAT HAPPENS NEXT?

Now that you have explored your triggers, it's time to learn what to do when they come up. Sometimes you can keep them from happening. For example, if you know that being hungry is a trigger, you can ask an adult for a snack. Other times you cannot keep the trigger from happening. If you know that one of your triggers is taking a test, what do you do if you have a spelling test on Friday? You may not be able to avoid the test. However, you can try your best to prepare.

First, describe your triggers in more detail. Where do they happen? Who is present when they happen? What are you doing when they happen? In the first column, list your triggers in detail. Make a list of how you might avoid those triggers in the second column. In the last column, write about what you might do if you can't avoid the trigger.

MY TRIGGER	HOW I CAN AVOID IT	HOW I CAN PREPARE FOR IT

MY TRIGGER	HOW I CAN AVOID IT	HOW I CAN PREPARE FOR IT

MY ATTITUDE

There are three main ways we communicate with other people. There is a passive way, an aggressive way, and an assertive way.

Passive communication is when someone avoids expressing themselves in an honest and clear manner. For example, imagine you and a friend are creating an art project together. Your friend asks you how you would like to create part of the project. A passive response might sound like saying, "Whatever you think is best."

Aggressive communication is when you express your own point of view without thinking of others. If you use this style, you might be loud, firm, or have a harsh tone of voice. An example of aggressive communication would be saying, "This is all your fault!"

Assertive communication allows you to make sure your own needs are taken care of while also respecting the other person. You might be calm while talking, use a warm voice, and feel confident about saying "I." An assertive statement might sound like saying, "I understand you would like me to lead this project, but I would like to share the work."

Think about your own behavior and how you communicate. Are you more passive, more aggressive, or more assertive?

COMMUNICATION STYLES

Review the chart to learn more about the three communication styles. Then read the statements and circle the matching communication style.

PASSIVE	AGGRESSIVE	ASSERTIVE
Has a soft or quiet tone of voice.	Has a loud, firm, or harsh tone of voice.	Is calm, wise, and respectful of others.
Usually has their head down or shoulders slouched.	Sometimes uses threats.	Expresses feelings.
Makes limited eye contact.	Puts other people down.	Is honest and confident.
Says they're sorry a lot.	Likes to be "right."	

continued »»

1. "I'm not cleaning my room because I don't want to!"

   AGGRESSIVE   PASSIVE   ASSERTIVE

2. "I can't play outside today. I have to finish my homework. Could we play another time?"

   AGGRESSIVE   PASSIVE   ASSERTIVE

3. "I let Johnny cheat off my math homework, and I'll feel bad if I make him stop. I'm not going to say anything."

   AGGRESSIVE   PASSIVE   ASSERTIVE

4. "You were late picking me up, and now I don't want to go with you!"

   AGGRESSIVE   PASSIVE   ASSERTIVE

5. "I feel sad when I come home to find my dog chewing my shoe."

   AGGRESSIVE   PASSIVE   ASSERTIVE

6. "I wish someone would remember to make my snack."

   AGGRESSIVE   PASSIVE   ASSERTIVE

WHAT DO I DO?

Now that you know more about communication styles, take this quiz to discover how you communicate. Read the following questions, and circle the response that you feel matches your style.

1. **How do you feel when you tell other people what you think?**

   a. I am fearful that others will be mad at me.

   b. I do not care what other people think.

   c. I am comfortable and look forward to hearing what other people think.

2. **Do you like being the center of attention?**

   a. Never!

   b. Always!

   c. I like when I can share the attention with others.

3. **Are you comfortable sharing your feelings with others?**

   a. No. I do not want people to know how I really feel.

   b. Yes. I like talking about myself and getting attention.

   c. Yes. I am confident in myself.

continued »»

4. **Do you like to be in charge and be the boss?**

   a. No. It is too much pressure.

   b. Yes! I like telling people what to do, even if they don't like it.

   c. If I am in charge, I like to make sure others feel respected.

5. **How do you listen to your friends' stories?**

   a. I listen, but I do not respond.

   b. I get bored and interrupt them.

   c. I listen in a respectful way.

6. **Are you ever rude to your friends?**

   a. Sometimes, when they think I am too quiet or ignoring them.

   b. Often.

   c. Rarely.

7. **Do you like to share your thoughts with your friends and family?**

   a. No. People do not care about my thoughts.

   b. Yes. I always say what I am thinking, even if it is not respectful.

c. Yes. It helps build relationships with the people I care about.

8. How do you communicate with grown-ups?

a. I am scared of grown-ups and avoid communicating with them.

b. I yell at grown-ups, because they always try to tell me what to do.

c. I try to be honest and respectful.

Now tally up your score.

As _____

Bs _____

Cs _____

If you answered mostly As, you tend to have a passive communication style.

If you answered mostly Bs, you tend to have an aggressive communication style.

If you answered mostly Cs, you tend to have an assertive communication style.

CHAPTER 3

Boosting My Self-Esteem

NOBODY IS PERFECT

No one in the world is perfect. You can be talented at something but still have struggles. Take Michael Jordan, for example. He is a legendary basketball player. But did you know that when he first tried out for the basketball team in high school, he didn't make the cut? This early setback didn't stop him. He loved the game and kept practicing every day. He went on to become one of the greatest players of all time. But even Michael Jordan isn't perfect. Aiming for perfection can be very dangerous.

When you try to be perfect, you spend all your time and energy focused on that one thing. It may cause you to neglect other areas in your life. This can be harmful to your self-esteem. When you are trying to become good at a skill, it doesn't happen overnight. Michael Jordan didn't become good at basketball overnight. He worked hard to boost his talent. If you have a skill that you want to improve, remember that it is okay to take breaks. If it becomes too much, take a step back, take a deep breath, and try again. Aim at improving your skill, not perfecting it.

WHAT MAKES ME UNIQUE

Everyone has things that make them unique. You might have a certain skill that makes you stand out. You could be an amazing artist. Maybe you are really good at skating. Or maybe you stand out because of your really cool haircut.

Trace your hand with your favorite color. Then write your name on the wrist of the drawing. On each of the fingers, write or draw something that makes you special. Continue to decorate the picture in a unique way.

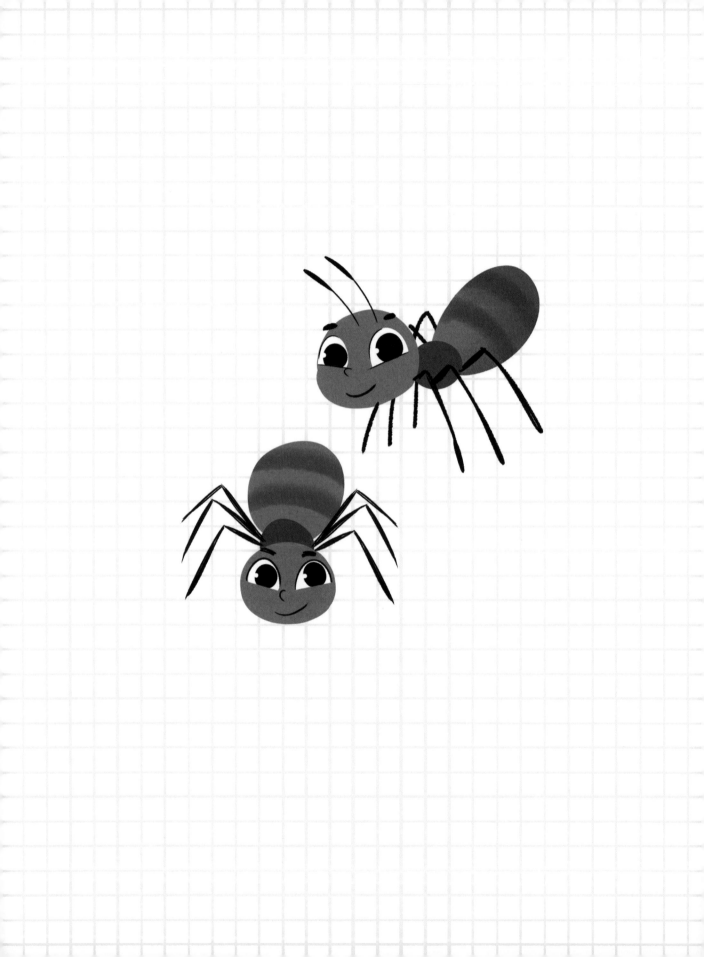

QUIETING NEGATIVE THOUGHTS

Our minds can sometimes play tricks on us. They can make us think negative or unhelpful thoughts about ourselves that are not true. Having a not-so-good feeling will sometimes make those negative thoughts *seem* like the truth. This also happens if you have unhealthy self-esteem.

Imagine you are having lunch with your friend at school. You always sit next to each other at lunchtime. What if your friend decided to sit somewhere else one day? How would that make you feel? You might feel sad or hurt. Maybe it leads to a bad thought about yourself. Were you not a good friend? Did you do something wrong? If you keep thinking like this, it leads to not-so-good feelings.

When you have a bad thought, try to tell that thought to stop or go away. Then tell yourself that the thought is not true. Once you recognize the bad thought, think about how it makes you feel. Does it make you feel sad? Hurt? Angry? Name the feeling and say it out loud. You can also share your emotion with a friend or grown-up. Try the next exercise to recognize your own negative thoughts and the feelings attached to them.

ANTS

Let's go, ANTs!

Sometimes when things happen to us, we think a negative or bad thought about ourselves. This can be known as an ANT! ANT stands for Automatic Negative Thought. ANTs will sometimes pop into our mind to tell us bad things about ourselves. To change a negative thought and boost your self-esteem, it helps to first know what the ANT is saying.

Think of a time when you may have felt overwhelmed, anxious, or sad. Write about what happened.

---

continued »»

Now think about an ANT you may have experienced during this time. What could you say to make that thought go away?

SETTING AND ACCOMPLISHING GOALS

Building your confidence takes time. It's not going to magically happen overnight. Start boosting your confidence by setting small goals. A goal is something that you wish to accomplish. When setting goals, you do not want them to be too large. Break up your goals into smaller steps. Say your goal is to read one book that is not assigned by your teacher. Set yourself the smaller goal of reading one chapter every day. If your goal is to save money to buy a skateboard, break that down to saving five dollars of your allowance each week. When you're figuring out how to set small goals, try to be SMART. SMART stands for:

continued »»

SPECIFIC:
You understand exactly what your goal is.

MEASURABLE:
You can tell how close you are to your goal.

ATTAINABLE:
You know you can make your goal happen.

RELEVANT:
The goal is part of something bigger you want for yourself.

TIME-BOUND:
You know roughly how much time it will take to achieve this goal.

Think about a goal you would like to set for yourself. Remember the SMART tool and what it stands for. Is it a SMART goal? In the next few exercises, you will start creating your own goals and developing your own action plan to achieve them.

GOAL SETTING

Take your time when you set your goals. You are not expected to list them all right away. Think about some things that you would like to change in your life. How would you change them? When would you like to have them changed by? When setting goals, there are a few things to remember.

→ Make your goal realistic. You want to be able to accomplish your goal without letting yourself down.

→ Make it hard, but not too hard! When setting a goal, you want to make it challenging, but you also don't want to make it too difficult.

→ Set a timeline. It can be unrealistic to expect that you'll achieve your goal tomorrow. Be mindful that it does take time to meet goals.

continued »»

Answer the following questions to help you create your goals.

1. **What is something you want to accomplish in the next week?**

   ----

2. **What is something you want to accomplish in the next month?**

   ----

3. **What is something you want to accomplish in the next year?**

   ----

4. **What items do you need to be able to meet your goals?**

   ----

5. **Who can help you meet your goals?**

MY ACTION PLAN

Once you have named your goals, you're ready to set an action plan! Remember to think of SMART when creating this plan. Is the goal *specific* to your need? Is the goal *measurable* or doable? Is the goal *attainable*? Is it *relevant* to your larger goal? How much *time* will you spend on this goal?

If you had a goal to study for your math test every night, your action plan might look like this:

1. **Keep all math materials at my study space.**

2. **Set an alarm as a reminder to study.**

3. **Ask an adult for support when I need it.**

Now it's your turn! Create an action plan to meet one of your goals.

My Goal: _____

_____

_____

continued »»

My Action Plan:

LOVING MYSELF

It's important to feel good about yourself. The best way to do this is to care for yourself and love yourself. Do things that bring you joy, like eating your favorite meal or playing on your favorite jungle gym. Another way to care for and love yourself is to think a nice thought. Give yourself a compliment, or tell yourself you did a great job at something.

Sometimes it can be hard to remember those nice things about ourselves. Sometimes it doesn't feel believable. Even on those hard days, it can be helpful to give yourself a compliment. Take some sticky notes or even a few small pieces of paper. Write down all the compliments you can think of to give yourself. Hang them up on your bathroom mirror, somewhere in your bedroom, or in a place where you go often. The important part is to read those statements every day and remember those kind thoughts or compliments. After you hang up your sticky notes, answer the questions on the next page to reflect on your experience.

1. Where did you place your sticky notes?

   _____

2. How did you feel before writing the notes?

   _____

3. What were some compliments you wrote on your notes?

   _____

4. How many days per week did you review your notes?

   _____

5. How did you feel after writing the notes?

   _____

A COMPLIMENT GOES A LONG WAY

One of the first steps to loving yourself is being able to say nice things about yourself. When you give yourself a compliment, it boosts your self-esteem. Write some compliments to yourself. Try to fill both pages!

YOUR BEST SELF

You might have a quality that you like more than other qualities. It could be your style, your hair, or your creativity. When you recognize what you love about yourself, you're then able to strengthen that quality. What do you like about yourself? What are you really good at? Draw a picture of yourself showing your best quality.

CHEERING MYSELF ON

Imagine you are at a football game. You're in the stands with your family and friends. You look out on the field, and the football teams are trying their best. Then you notice that on the sidelines there are people in uniforms cheering the teams on. Those people are *cheerleaders*. The cheerleaders' job is to encourage their team.

Just like the football players, we need cheerleaders in our life as well. That doesn't mean someone follows us around, shaking pom-poms and cheering at us throughout the day. That would be a bit silly. You can be your own cheerleader, though! Football players might feel sad, upset, or frustrated on the field if they're losing the game. But when they hear cheerleaders and the crowd supporting them, they feel encouraged. Cheer yourself on by saying positive and encouraging statements. You could say, "I'm doing my best," "I am loved," or "I am valued." These are called *affirmations*. You can think affirmations in your head or say them out loud. Boost your self-esteem in the next few exercises by learning more about affirmations.

AFFIRMATIONS ON THE GO

Affirmations are positive statements that you can use throughout the day to remind yourself that you are awesome. When you write an affirmation down, you can keep it in a special place or hang it up in your bedroom. But you can also take it with you anywhere! Just keep it handy in your backpack, your pocket, or a notebook. Complete the sentences on the next page to start your very own list of affirmations.

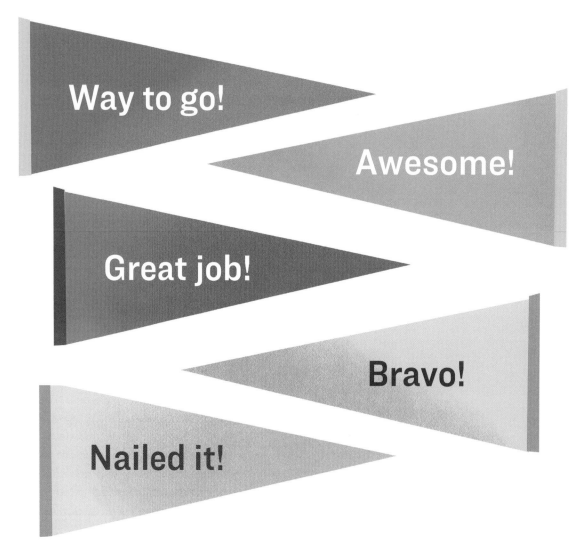

I am -

I welcome -

I choose -

I believe -

I have -

I love -

I feel -

I know -

POSITIVE BREATHING

Remember the bubble breathing you practiced earlier? (Turn to page 36 if you need a refresher!) Taking a deep breath in and then slowly blowing your air out helps you relax and calm down, and it improves your mood. For this exercise, practice deep bubble breathing. This time, however, take a pause every time you breathe in. Think about one affirmation you listed in the previous exercise. Then breathe out like you are blowing a bubble.
Do this until you have made it through your list of positive affirmations.

How did you feel before your bubble breathing? How do you feel after breathing with affirmations? Take a moment to reflect on your experience. Write about your feelings and note whether they changed.

continued »»

Did your feelings change after your bubble breathing? Use the space below to draw how you felt after the bubble breathing exercise.

What other affirmations do you think would help you? Draw more bubbles in the space below and write your affirmations inside them.

CHAPTER 4

Finding My Voice

RECOGNIZING ASSERTIVENESS

Assertiveness is a way of communicating how you feel. It can also be a way to communicate your thoughts and opinions. Being assertive boosts self-esteem. When you are assertive, you are confident about saying your feelings and needs. You are standing up for yourself. You are also showing respect for other people's feelings.

If you are using assertive communication, you try to make eye contact with the person you are talking to. You speak with a confident tone. You hold yourself upright, but not in a stiff way. Communicating like this has many benefits. When you are assertive, you express how you really feel, and you're not afraid to stand up for your beliefs.

Have you ever been bullied, or do you know someone who has been bullied? Standing up to bullies is hard! However, if you practice assertive communication, you will be able to share your wants, needs, and opinions when standing up to someone. Assertiveness offers bully protection. If you want to be more assertive, start practicing today. Go to a mirror and try to make eye contact, stand upright, and state how you feel. The more you practice looking in the mirror and stating your feelings, the better you will become at assertiveness.

BEING ASSERTIVE

Think about someone in your life who shows assertiveness. What do you notice about this person when you spend time with them? Answer the questions to describe this person.

What actions does this person do?

How does this person talk?

Does this person share or hide their feelings?

Do you think this person has healthy or unhealthy self-esteem?

How do you feel about this person?

What about this person makes you feel that way?

TRUSTING MYSELF

Sometimes when people make a mistake, they have trouble trusting themselves. Once you lose trust in yourself, it might lower your self-esteem. Sometimes you may even quit or stop an activity that you once enjoyed. The truth is, learning to trust yourself is hard. Even adults struggle with trusting themselves sometimes.

Trusting yourself is listening to your inner voice. It is having thoughts, feelings, and opinions—and believing them. When you trust yourself, you have full confidence in your choices. Do you remember the first time you were dropped off at school? It may have been a bit scary, because you didn't know what to expect. But then maybe you walked right up to the building and went into class with confidence. This is you trusting yourself. You may have been nervous or uneasy, but you went in and got to know your teacher and your classmates.

Have you ever been given a job or task by your teacher? Maybe you're a line leader, in charge of sharpening the pencils, or even sent to deliver messages to the front office. If you believe in yourself, you will be able to do the job in a confident way. But how do you know when you believe in yourself? The next exercise will help you figure it out.

DRAWING TRUST

How do you know when you trust in yourself? You probably have confidence in your abilities without even realizing it. Think about it. Maybe you feel confident when riding your bike. You may be the first kid to raise your hand in class to answer a question. This is trusting yourself. Think about what trust means to you. Then write or draw what trusting in yourself means.

LEARNING TO SPEAK UP

Have you ever wanted to say something but were too scared or too worried about what might happen? How did it feel when you weren't able to speak your thoughts? Part of being assertive and building your self-esteem is learning to speak up for yourself. This can be pretty hard. Even grown-ups struggle with it at times. When you learn to trust yourself and your thoughts, speaking up becomes easier.

Do you feel confident speaking up in some places more than others? Speaking up at home might be easier than speaking up in class. Or it could be the opposite for you. Maybe you are in class, and your teacher puts a math question on the board. The teacher asks whether anyone has the answer. You think you might know the answer, so you raise your hand and speak up. This is healthy self-esteem and being able to trust yourself.

To build the skill of speaking up, practice saying how you feel before you give a thought. Try to use "I feel" statements. If your friend accidentally says something hurtful, you could say, "I feel sad that you called me that name" or "I feel hurt by what you said." In the next few exercises, practice different ways of speaking up.

I FEEL

Remember, only *you* get to choose how you feel. This is something that you control. No one else can tell you how you should feel. Other people's actions may lead you to feel hurt, but only you can choose whether you are sad or angry about it. Your feelings are your choice. When you speak to someone about your feelings, it can be helpful to use an "I feel" statement. Here are some examples.

"I feel sad that you didn't sit with me at lunch."

"I feel angry that you skipped me in the lunch line."

"I felt hurt when you didn't say good morning like you always do."

For this exercise, complete the sentences below.

1. **I feel** _ **when** _ _ _ _ _ _ _ _ _ _ _ _ _ _ _ _ _ _

    _

2. **I feel** _ **when** _ _ _ _ _ _ _ _ _ _ _ _ _ _ _ _ _

    _

3. **I feel** _ **when** _ _ _ _ _ _ _ _ _ _ _ _ _ _ _ _ _

    _

FEEL YOUR FEELINGS

Have you ever noticed how your emotions show up in your body? When you're angry, you might feel your face get hot, your hands might get sweaty, or you might even clench your teeth. Draw a line from each emotion below to the part of the body where you usually feel that emotion.

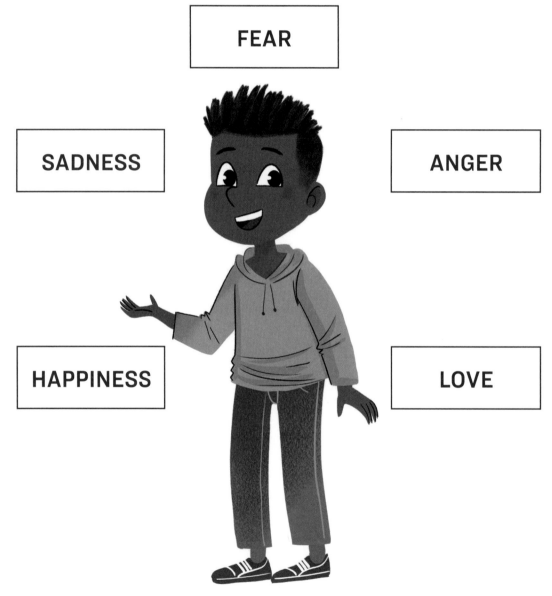

FEAR

SADNESS

ANGER

HAPPINESS

LOVE

IT'S OKAY TO SAY NO

Sometimes things will happen that make you feel uncomfortable. When those things happen, it can be scary to stand up for yourself and speak your mind. One of the hardest things to do is to say no. Disagreeing is not a bad thing. You have the right to say no to things that don't make you feel comfortable. You have the right to be treated with respect and to stand up for yourself.

Imagine you and your friend are playing outside. Your parent told you to stay on the playground and to avoid going into the woods nearby. However, your friend tells you it would be fun to explore the woods when your parent isn't looking. This is a good time to say no. It is you standing up for what you feel is right and what feels comfortable. Practice saying no in front of a mirror. Say it loudly, clearly, and confidently. The more you practice, the more confident you will be when you have to say no in a real situation.

SAYING NO FOR YOURSELF

Have you ever been in a situation where you wanted to say no but couldn't? Maybe you had a friend ask you to do something when you really didn't want to. Maybe you felt like you had to do what they asked because they were your friend. Being able to say no and speak your mind is a big part of healthy self-esteem.

Write or draw about a time that you wanted to say no but ended up saying yes instead. Then answer the questions.

How did it make you feel to say yes when you wanted to say no? - - - - - - -

- -

- -

- -

Now imagine you did say no. How would that make you feel? - - - - - - - - - -

- -

- -

- -

How do you think it would make the other person feel? - - - - - - - - - - - - - -

- -

- -

- -

TRACKING YOUR PROGRESS

Now you have a better sense of when to say no and how to speak up for yourself. To build this skill, you have to put it into practice. Remember it's not about just saying no—it's about saying what you really want to do. If your friend or an adult in your life asks you to do something and you really don't want to, you should feel confident in speaking your mind. For the next week, reference this chart. Check off every day you spoke your mind, said no when you needed to, and shared your feelings.

Monday	☐ I spoke my mind. ☐ I said no when I needed to. ☐ I shared my feelings.
Tuesday	☐ I spoke my mind. ☐ I said no when I needed to. ☐ I shared my feelings.
Wednesday	☐ I spoke my mind. ☐ I said no when I needed to. ☐ I shared my feelings.

Thursday	☐ I spoke my mind. ☐ I said no when I needed to. ☐ I shared my feelings.
Friday	☐ I spoke my mind. ☐ I said no when I needed to. ☐ I shared my feelings.
Saturday	☐ I spoke my mind. ☐ I said no when I needed to. ☐ I shared my feelings.
Sunday	☐ I spoke my mind. ☐ I said no when I needed to. ☐ I shared my feelings.

TALKING TIPS

Think about how you speak to others. When you are talking to your teachers, parents, and friends, are you confident in your words? When you are speaking to other people, there are a few important things to keep in mind.

When you are talking to someone, speak clearly and confidently. When you share your thoughts and feelings with someone, it can boost your self-esteem. If you are unsure of what to say, trusting yourself will boost your confidence. Don't put too much thought into it. Just go with your gut. Your inner voice is usually right and can be helpful to follow when you feel uneasy or unsure.

Remember that it is okay to say no. Stand up for yourself. If your friend asks you to stop what you're doing to come play with them, be confident in saying no if you don't want to play. Tell them you would rather continue your activity.

Consider these tips when you talk to others.

1. **Trust yourself.**

2. **When in doubt, go with your gut.**

3. **Use "I feel" statements to speak up for yourself.**

4. **Speak clearly and confidently.**

5. **Say what you mean and mean what you say.**

6. Say no without feeling guilty.

7. Speak up for yourself and others.

8. Sit or stand up straight.

9. Start small.

10. Practice what you want to say.

POSITIVE COMMUNICATION

If you are working on building your self-esteem, an important part is communication. You want to be positive and assertive. Remember that assertive communication means standing up for yourself and sharing how you feel in a respectful manner. When you use assertive communication, your friends and grown-ups will be able to understand how you are feeling. If they understand how you are feeling, they can support you and help you with what you need. Read the sentences below. Check off each example of assertive communication.

- ☐ Chris pushes Lauren because she called him a bad name.

- ☐ Kelly asks, "Zoey, can you please stop throwing the ball at me?"

- ☐ Amy is mad at Julie for making fun of her, but she doesn't say anything to her.

- ☐ Josh is angry at his brother, so he sneaks into his room and breaks his toy.

- ☐ Sarah doesn't let Christian play her game because she is mad at him.

- ☐ Hannah says, "I need you to please stop calling me names behind my back."

- ☐ Christina is mad at Lesley, so she counts to 10 before expressing her feelings.

☐ Kimberly tells Jess that she's the "worst friend in the world!"

☐ Taylor says, "I am tired of you picking on me. It hurts my feelings."

☐ Amanda pulls Paul to the side and asks him to be nicer to her.

SELF-PORTRAIT

What does being assertive look like? When someone is assertive, you might notice more than just their words. They have confidence in what they are saying, and you can see it in their body language. They may be standing up tall, looking you in the eyes, and keeping their voice at a good volume.

Think about what you look like when you are using assertive language. How would your friends describe you when you are assertive with them? Do you stand up straight? What is your facial expression? What kind of tone do you use when you speak? Draw a picture of what you would look like using assertive communication.

CHAPTER 5

Self-Esteem and My Life

FAMILY MATTERS

In the last chapter you learned about using "I feel" statements with your friends. You can also use these statements when communicating with your family. Letting your family know how you feel can be a nice way to connect with them for support.

When you are experiencing unhealthy self-esteem, it can also affect your family life. It isn't just a problem in the outside world. If you live in a home with siblings or other children your age, there might be times when they come into your space. There might be moments when you have to share things when you don't really want to. If this happens, it might make you feel unheard, sad, or even frustrated. Communicating your "I feel" statement to a trusted adult can help. If the adult doesn't know how you are feeling, they may not know how they can help. When you communicate your feelings to your family, it forms a stronger relationship and will also boost your self-esteem.

MY HOME

You should feel comfortable at home. Your family can make you feel safe and secure. When things happen at home, you can let your family know how you feel. The power of an "I feel" statement goes a long way. To feel comfortable communicating this way, you have to be able to trust the adults in your life.

Every family is unique. Families come in all shapes and sizes. Think about your family. Is your family supportive? Do they encourage you to do your best? Are you able to tell them how you feel? List the members of your family below, then draw a picture of your family on the next page. Include the things that make your family unique and special.

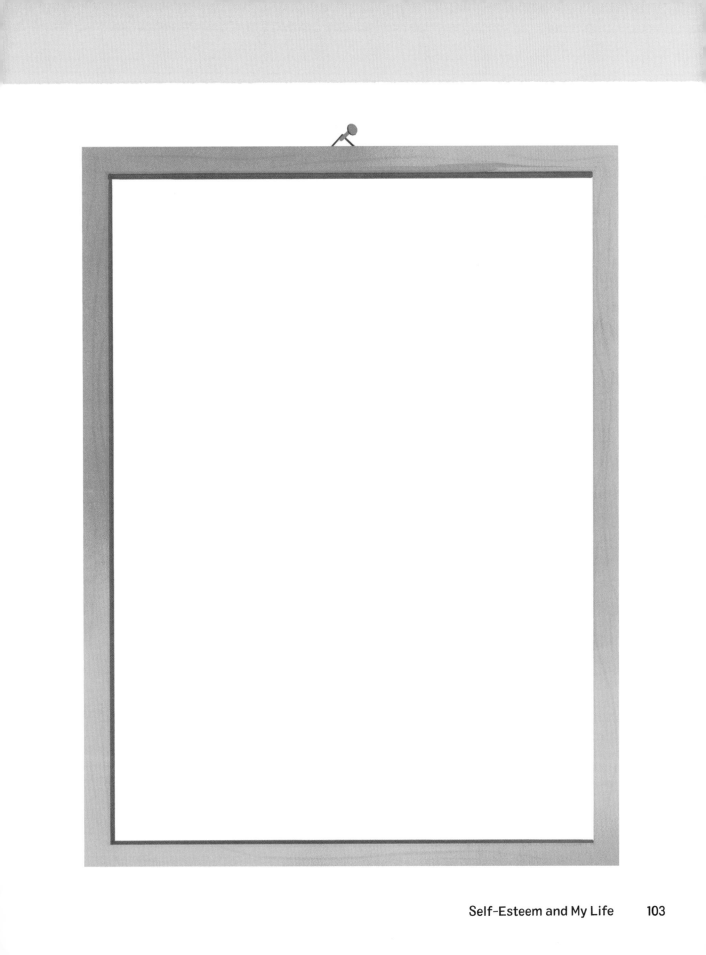

ME AND MY FRIENDS

Picture one of your friends. Who comes to mind? It could be someone from school, someone you ride the bus with, or someone in your neighborhood. What is the most important thing about your friendship with this person? It could be that your friend always remembers things about you. Or that you can always count on them to be there. Or even that you just have fun when you play together. These are all positive qualities that make a healthy friendship.

Sometimes you may experience a friendship that is not so good. How do you know if a friendship is not healthy? First, it's important to understand what you value in a friend. If you have an unhealthy friendship, your friend might be unkind to you. They might not include you in events. They might sit with you at lunch one day but then ignore you the next day. These kinds of friendships can be hard. There might be times when you aren't quite sure what to do. When you are looking for healthy friendships, remember to find friends who make you feel good. These friends are going to enjoy spending time with you, talking to you, playing with you, and being there for you.

HEALTHY OR UNHEALTHY FRIENDSHIP

Sometimes it can be hard to tell whether a friendship is healthy or unhealthy. Think about what makes a good friend for you.

EXAMPLE OF HEALTHY FRIENDSHIP

You left your snack at home, so Hannah shared her lunch with you.

EXAMPLE OF UNHEALTHY FRIENDSHIP

Leah laughed at you when you tripped and fell in the hallway.

For each of the following sentences, circle whether it is part of a healthy or unhealthy friendship.

1. **Cait told you she liked your outfit.**

   HEALTHY FRIENDSHIP   UNHEALTHY FRIENDSHIP

2. **Mariah invited you over to play after school.**

   HEALTHY FRIENDSHIP   UNHEALTHY FRIENDSHIP

3. Jeremy cut in front of you in line at the water fountain.

   HEALTHY FRIENDSHIP   UNHEALTHY FRIENDSHIP

4. Heather gave everyone an invitation to her birthday party except you.

   HEALTHY FRIENDSHIP   UNHEALTHY FRIENDSHIP

5. You were playing by yourself when Lauren came to play with you.

   HEALTHY FRIENDSHIP   UNHEALTHY FRIENDSHIP

6. Chris picked you to be on his team in gym class.

   HEALTHY FRIENDSHIP   UNHEALTHY FRIENDSHIP

7. You were struggling with a math problem when Sarah offered some help.

   HEALTHY FRIENDSHIP   UNHEALTHY FRIENDSHIP

8. Milly told you not to play with her and her friends.

   HEALTHY FRIENDSHIP   UNHEALTHY FRIENDSHIP

HANDLING CONFLICT

Imagine that you and your best friend are on the playground. You really wanted to swing in the red swing, but your friend insisted that was their swing. You tell them that you were there first and you really wanted to try that swing, but they still insist that they should go first. Now you are upset because you disagree with your friend. You want to keep playing with them, but it was your turn on the swing. This is called *conflict*. Conflict is when you and another person disagree. You can have conflict with your family, friends, and even pets.

Self-esteem has a big role in handling conflict. People with healthy self-esteem handle conflict better than those with unhealthy self-esteem. Conflict can cause you to feel like you are alone. It can also create feelings like guilt and shame. These feelings make it hard for you and your friend to settle the conflict. This is when you become less confident in yourself and your decisions. On the one hand, you want to keep playing with your friend. But on the other, you know it is really your turn on the swing. How do you handle this? What would you say to your friend? You could let your friend know how you feel. You could ask your friend to choose something else to play, like going down the slide or playing on the jungle gym.

One way to resolve a conflict is to meet in the middle. If your friend still insists it is their turn, play with something else and come back to the swings later. It's not always easy, but with practice and experience it will get better.

WHAT IS CONFLICT?

Have you ever experienced conflict with someone? Sometimes conflict can be a misunderstanding. Or maybe there is a miscommunication. Write about a time that you had conflict with someone.

What did you do?

What did that person say to you?

What did you do to resolve the conflict?

Are you still friends with this person?

How did you feel after the conflict?

WISE CHOICES

There are many things you can do when you have conflict. The important part is knowing what choices are wise. When you make a choice, there is always an outcome. If you make a wise choice, it is more likely you will have a positive outcome. If you make a not-so-wise choice, then you may have a negative outcome.

Read through the following choices. Put a checkmark next to the wise choices you could make if you were facing conflict with someone.

- ☐ Tell yourself that you are capable and strong and you can handle it.

- ☐ Ignore the person.

- ☐ Yell at the person to go away.

- ☐ Use breathing techniques to help manage your feelings.

- ☐ Tell a trusted adult, like a teacher, parent, or friend.

- ☐ Throw something at the person.

- ☐ Tell the person how they are hurting your feelings.

- ☐ Respond to the person by giving them a compliment.

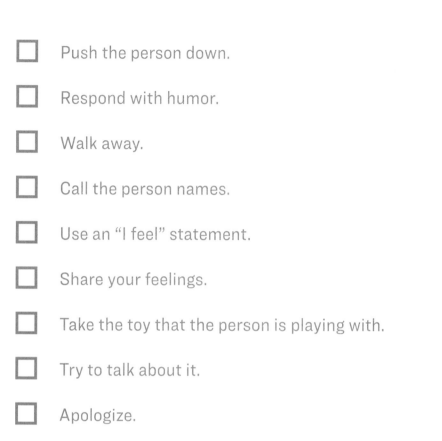

☐   Push the person down.

☐   Respond with humor.

☐   Walk away.

☐   Call the person names.

☐   Use an "I feel" statement.

☐   Share your feelings.

☐   Take the toy that the person is playing with.

☐   Try to talk about it.

☐   Apologize.

EMBRACING EMPATHY

You know the importance of communicating your feelings to others. Sharing your feelings helps people understand how they can help you. But how do you understand other people's feelings? You offer something called *empathy.* Empathy is something that lives inside us. It is a caring emotion. It is the ability to put yourself in someone else's shoes. Once you take a walk in someone else's shoes, you can start to understand what they are feeling.

Imagine seeing your friend carrying their lunch tray when they trip and spill all their food. You might feel empathy toward them, because you can relate to their sense of sadness. You might even feel a little bit of sadness yourself. Your feeling of sadness is you showing empathy.

Empathy can be shown with other emotions, too. You can show empathy for happiness, anger, or fear. The next few exercises are going to help you use empathy.

OFFERING EMPATHY

You can offer empathy to your friends, family, teachers, and parents. This will help you build strong relationships throughout your life. Answer these questions to explore empathy.

1. Describe a time when you felt empathy toward someone else.

   ----

2. What do you think is the purpose of empathy?

   ----

3. What are some ways that you can show that you care for others?

USING EMPATHY

Have you ever walked in someone else's shoes?
If you literally put on someone else's shoes, you
might notice they are too tight or too large for you.
This is kind of like empathy. You are feeling what
that person feels.

Read about the following people. Think about the
situation each person is in. Then answer the questions to practice
showing empathy.

Gage forgot to study for his math test.

How do you think he is feeling? -

Have you ever felt this way? -

When you felt this way, what helped you feel better? - - - - - - - - -

- -

What would you say to Gage to help him feel better? - - - - - - - - -

- -

Kristen's dog ran away at the park.

How do you think she is feeling? -

Have you ever felt this way? -

When you felt this way, what helped you feel better? - - - - - - - - - -

- -

What would you say to Kristen to help her feel better? - - - - - - - - - -

- -

Chris answered a question wrong in front of the entire class. Then the class laughed at him.

How do you think he is feeling? -

Have you ever felt this way? -

What would you say to Chris to help him feel better? - - - - - - - - - -

- -

CHOOSING GOOD

When you are having a positive day, do you feel good? Probably. When you are having a negative day, do you feel not so good? Maybe. Positivity goes a long way. When you are having a positive day or something positive happens to you, you will usually experience good feelings. When you are being positive and have positive thoughts, it can make you feel better about yourself. It can make you feel more comfortable in the world. It can strengthen your relationships.

Even on hard days, there are things you can do to make yourself smile and be more positive. You can talk about your feelings with a friend or a trusted adult. You can do something that you enjoy, like taking a walk, playing with your favorite toy, or listening to your favorite song. This might help you smile and be more positive.

Last, it is important to celebrate your victories. If you made it through a rough day, congratulate yourself. You did it! Make your own list of things that make you happy and help you feel good about yourself. Then use the list whenever you're struggling with self-esteem.

OCEAN BREATHING

Part of boosting your self-esteem is making healthy choices and taking care of yourself. Breathing is a simple way to take care of yourself. One helpful way of breathing is called *ocean breathing*.

Find a comfortable place to sit. It could be in a chair or on the floor with a pillow. Now take a deep breath through your nose. When you breathe out, pretend you are blowing the air through a straw. When you are breathing slowly and steadily like this, it sounds like the ocean waves crashing on the shore.

Try this exercise three more times. Then reflect on your experience by answering these questions.

How did it make you feel? _____

_____

_____

When would you use ocean breathing? _____

_____

_____

How often would you use ocean breathing? _____

_____

BODY SQUEEZING

Body squeezing can create the feeling of relaxation. When you practice squeezing parts of your body, it sends a message to your brain to feel relaxed and calm. Have you ever felt a big emotion like anger or frustration? When you are able to tune in to the present moment by body squeezing, it will help you handle the situation better. By learning how to handle frustrating situations better, you are also creating healthy self-esteem. For this exercise, you are going to relax and squeeze each muscle in your body, one by one. Once you are finished, answer the questions.

1. Start with your toes. Curl your toes as tight as you can, as if they are holding a pencil. Count to five. Now drop the pencil and relax your toes.

2. Tense up your legs as tight as you can, as if you are standing on your toes. Count to five and then relax your legs.

3. Suck in your stomach, as if you are sliding into a tight space. Count to five and then release your stomach.

4. Make fists with your hands as tight as you can. Count to five and then release your fists.

5. Scrunch up your nose. Count to five and then release.

How did this exercise make you feel afterward?

Are there any parts of the exercise you could practice at school?

When would you practice body squeezing?

EVERYDAY TOOLS

. . . .

Congratulations! You finished the activities in this book. Building self-esteem takes time, so the work isn't over. Here are some fun bonus techniques you can use in your everyday practice. Keep at it. You're amazing!

Coping Words

Sometimes when you feel big feelings, they take over and turn into big reactions. Those reactions can be negative and harmful. If this happens, try to use coping words. Coping words can be a phrase or statement that you say to bring comfort. It makes you feel better. Next time you experience not-so-good feelings, try repeating these coping words to yourself: "I am safe. I am here."

Light It Up

When you walk into a room and turn on the lights, what happens? It gets bright. The lights are designed to brighten the room so we can see. Just like light bulbs, you can also shine. When you are in a room, take a look around. How many light bulbs do you see? For every light bulb you count in the room, think of one nice thing to say about yourself. So, if there are five light bulbs, say five nice things about yourself.

Candy Thoughts

Do you enjoy candy? Believe it or not, this sweet treat can help you build your self-esteem! Put a piece of candy in your mouth, but do not chew or swallow it yet! Hold the candy in your mouth for three minutes. Be still and quiet. Focus on the flavor, texture, and all other aspects of the candy. You may want to chew or swallow the candy, but resist the urge. When you focus on the candy, you are actually practicing a skill that helps when you feel not so good. Focus and calm will help boost your self-esteem.

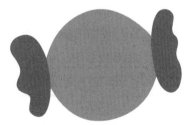

Gentle Stretching

Movement can help you feel centered. If you are experiencing big emotions or not-so-good feelings, sometimes moving your body will help get you back on track. Stand with your feet shoulder-distance apart and your arms by your sides. Lift your arms straight above your head and reach for the stars. Hold for ten seconds. Wiggle your toes and fingers. Now reach over and stretch as far as you can to see whether you can touch your toes. Return to the center and shake it out!

Gratitude Walk

Think about your day. What happened today that made you feel grateful? Maybe you can immediately list a few things. Maybe you are struggling to think of things and are feeling down. Try a gratitude walk when you are feeling down. Take a walk around your home or outside. For every step that you take, name something that you are grateful for.

MORE TO LEARN

. . . .

BOOKS

CBT Workbook for Kids: 40+ Fun Exercises and Activities to Help Children Overcome Anxiety & Face Their Fears at Home, at School, and Out in the World by Heather Davidson, Psy.D BCN. Callisto Publishing, 2019. This workbook uses cognitive behavioral therapy strategies to help kids manage worries and feel more confident in any situation.

Empowered Girls: Activities and Affirmations for Empowering Strong, Confident Girls by Allison Kimmey. Rockridge Press, 2021. This book features activities and affirmations to inspire girls to feel confident and empowered.

Executive Functioning Workbook for Kids: 40 Fun Activities to Build Memory, Flexible Thinking, and Self-Control Skills at Home, in School, and Beyond by Sharon Grand. Callisto Kids, 2021. This workbook uses hands-on activities to help kids improve the everyday skills involved in memory, organization, and paying attention. Kids will feel inspired to develop their skills and talents and feel more confident as a result.

WEBSITES

Gabriel Araujo, "Your Child's Self-Esteem," kidshealth.org/en/parents /self-esteem.html. Nemours KidsHealth is a website for parents, kids, teens, and educators. You'll find tips for parents and educators on how to talk with children to help boost their confidence. There are also quizzes, expert Q&As, and videos for kids and teens that help explain self-esteem building.

Courtney E. Ackerman, "18 Self-Esteem Worksheets and Activities," positivepsychology.com/self-esteem-worksheets. PositivePsychology.com provides worksheets, parenting tips, and other helpful links to help kids and adults build self-esteem.

Family Focus Blog, "List of Helpful Self Esteem Activities for Kids," familyfocusblog.com/how-to-help-kids-develop-good-self-esteem. This blog provides relational information for kids and their families to work together. It's full of fun activities to try together as a family. It's not only for building self-esteem but also for improving the overall relationship as a family.

Child Mind Institute, "12 Tips for Raising Confident Kids," childmind .org/article/12-tips-raising-confident-kids. This online resource is focused on parents. The Child Mind Institute provides a complete guide to coaching your child through challenging life stages. You can ask experts questions and receive personal responses. You can also sign up for their monthly newsletter.

ABOUT THE AUTHOR

 **TAIRA BURNS** was born and raised in the beautiful Smoky Mountains outside of Knoxville, Tennessee. She graduated from high school with high honors, then obtained her bachelor of arts in psychology at Tusculum College. While in college, Taira worked in internships involving children with autism spectrum disorder. She then earned her master of science in clinical mental health counseling. Taira spent her early career working with youths in the juvenile justice system and their families at a local community agency. Taira is a licensed professional counselor in the state of Tennessee. She now works in a private practice setting, specializing in children and teens with anxiety, depression, and school-transitioning issues. In her free time, she enjoys being outdoors, kayaking, hiking, and swimming with her husband and three dogs. Taira also creates mental health content on social media platforms, including TikTok and Instagram. She shares information on anxiety, boundary setting, and school-related issues. She has gained a following of over 45,000. Her handle is TairaTalksTherapy.